The Free and Hanseatic City of

HAMBURG

Illustrated Guide to the Historical Town Centre and surrounding area

KU-594-855

The view from Stintfang looking eastwards across Hamburg (J. Bundsen, 1825).

Text: Wolfgang Kootz
Photographs: Tanja Timm,
Ulrich Strauch, and others.

Published by Kraichgau Verlag

HAMBURG
Tourismus GmbH

Hamburg à la CARD

Freie Fahrt mit öffentlichen Verkehrsmitteln (HVV) im Großbereich Hamburg. | Spartarife bei Stadt-und Hafenrundfahrten, Alstertouren und vielen weiteren Sehenswürdigkeiten | Freier Eintritt oder ermäßigte Preise in vielen Museen.

Free Travel on public transportation (HVV) in Hamburg metropolitan area | Special Rates when exploring the city by excursion boat in the port, on the Alster Lake or on guided bus tours and when visiting many other sights | Free or reduced admission to many museums.

Preise | Prices

Preise gültig ab April 2006 | Prices effective as April 2006

Einzelkarten	Single Ticket	Gruppenkarten	Group Ticket
1 Erwachsener und bis zu 3 Kinder unter 15	1 adult ans max. 3 children up to age 15		bis zu 5 Personen beliebigen Alters	up to 5 persons any age	
**Tageskarte	Day Ticket € 7,80**		**Tageskarte	Day Ticket € 11,20**	
Mehrtageskarte		**Mehrtageskarte**	
Multi Day Ticket	**€ 17,40**	**Multi Day Ticket**	**€ 28,30**

Verkaufsstellen: Direkt in Hamburg in den Tourist Informationen, vielen Hotels, HVV- Servicestellen und Fahrkartenautomaten. Im Reisebüro über START/KART oder über die **Hamburg-Hotline +49-40/300 51 300**
Where to purchase the Hamburg CARD: At all Hamburg tourist information offices, in various hotels, at Hamburg Transit Authority (HVV) Customer Offices, ticket machines and on the **Hamburg Hotline +49-40/300 51 300**

Welcome to Hamburg!

It is with these words that the voice on the loudspeakers at Willkommhöft greet ships coming up-river to the Hamburg docks, and with the same words we would like to extend a hearty welcome to you, the reader of this small book. It is intended to help you to track down the tourist highlights in the welter of buildings of this huge city, with its 1.8 million inhabitants and an area of 755 square kilometres, and to fit each one into its historical context. The suggested walk through the city, starting at the mainline railway station, lasts about 4 hours (excluding visits to see the interiors of buildings), so the visitor should plan at least one break on the way round or else split the tour up into two or more sections. It is advisable to undertake the section west of the "Michel" separately, and to find out beforehand at what time the Reeperbahn really comes to life. Here, as in other trips to Hamburg's more distant suburbs, the dense network of public transport makes it easy to do without the car. A visit to Hamburg is of course not complete without a tour of the docks, passing numerous ships large and small, quays and landing bridges, and warehouses and dockyards, and which is available in all possible variations from a number of points along the north bank of the Elbe. Towering in the background are modern skyscrapers, the towers of the St Pauli landing bridges and the "Michel", and the unique "city" of warehouses, all forming the trade-mark of Hamburg's docklands. And it is from the deck of a boat crossing the Alster, the artificial lake and water-sports centre in the middle of the city, that the visitor can best enjoy the tower of the noble Rathaus [Town Hall]. The Alster, together with the Elbe and the numerous canals, and the parks adjoining them have given Hamburg the fine image of a "green" metropolis at the water's edge. A total of 2,321 bridges cross these canals, known here as Fleete - more bridges than any other city in the world possesses. Apart from this, Hamburg's reputation as a centre of culture and entertainment precedes it. In addition to countless houses of entertainment (of all kinds) in the Reeperbahn district, which never close, there are the world-famous Fischmarkt on Sunday mornings and the innumerable live-entertainment pubs, casinos, and shows, as well as the museums with world-famous exhibits and the city's famous theatres; they are the leaders in the whole German cultural scene because they are packed so full every night that they often do not need to change their programmes for years. Hamburg's negative image as a city in which everyone has to carry an umbrella is denied by the statistics; it does not rain any more frequently here than in Southern Germany, and the total hours of sunshine are above average. Nevertheless, urban planners and investors have created an impressive landscape of shopping streets with a veritable labyrinth of roofed-in shopping arcades which is the largest in terms of area in the whole of Germany. This contributes to making the Hanseatic city attractive for tourists at any time of year and regardless of the weather, and thus to the fact that more than 150,000 come every day. Hamburg is thus truly the Gateway to the World, a claim which the tourist trade always tries to live up to by offering both traditional German and international hotels and restaurants. As a centre of tourism, Hamburg offers the visitor an interesting range of packaged tours with a large number of different possible combinations, starting with the "Hamburg Card" and including visits to theatres, musical events, variety theatre, Hagenbeck's zoo, ship cruises to Heligoland, culinary journeys of exploration, or visits to the celebrations on New Year's Eve, Easter, and the "Harbour's Birthday". Although Hamburg is Germany's biggest industrial city, and although its centre was totally destroyed in the Great Fire of 1842 and again by bombing in 1943, it is an extraordinarily beautiful city and worth a visit at any time of year.

3

History of the city

Early 9th cent.	The "Hammaburg" is built to replace earlier fortifications and develops into a town-like trading centre ("Wik") and bishopric.
845	Vikings attack the town, and plunder and destroy the castle. The See is dissolved in 848.
10th cent.	Slav tribes overrun the region. Hamburg becomes the residence of the Dukes of Saxony.
11th cent.	Two castles are built opposite one another, the Alsterburg and the Neue Burg. Following further attacks by Slavs, the Dukes withdraw from Hamburg.
1189	The Emperor Friedrich Barbarossa grants the town exemption from customs duties and the right to govern trade throughout the Lower Elbe area, down to the estuary.
12th cent.	Hamburg is governed by the Counts of Schauenburg, who promote overseas trade. The "new" town with the St. Nicholas' church develops around the Neue Burg.
1201-27	Hamburg comes into the possession of the Danes. They unify the "old" and the "new" towns and in 1220 grant municipal rights to the settlements (population 1,500).
1227	The Danes are forced to retreat. New areas are settled. Hamburg takes on a special position in the Hansa trading league.
1284	Great Fire.
1359	Karl IV grants privileges: the city can bring pirates to trial, and earns universal gratitude by making sea routes safe from them. The Export brewery greatly strengthens Hamburg's trade.
1510	Hamburg now has some 13,000 inhabitants and is elevated to the rank of an Imperial City
1558	The first German stock exchange is founded, and the various dock towns are merged together into one commercial entity. The cloth trade blossoms.
1616-25	By building a huge system of fortifications, Hamburg is able to avoid the devastation of the 30 Years' War
1712	Plague kills 10,000 of the city's 70,000 inhabitants. The basis of a democratic constitution is created by the "Rezess".
End of 18th cent.	Poverty is widespread as Hamburg suffers from a weak economic position and various natural catastrophes.
1806-14	Hamburg under Napoleon's rule.
1815	The city enters the Deutscher Bund, an early form of federation, as a Free and Hanseatic City.

1842	Great Fire: 50% of the buildings are destroyed. The city is rebuilt along modern lines.
1867	The city enters the Norddeutscher Bund.
1881	Hamburg enters the Zollverein or Customs Union, a free-trade area covering most of northern Germany. The docklands are extended.
1892	A cholera epidemic causes 8,600 deaths. A new housing law allows the slums to be torn down.
1913	Hamburg has more than 1 million inhabitants.
1923	An attempted Putsch by a Communist leader, Ernst Thälmann, is put down by the police.
1937	The Greater Hamburg Law adds the present-day suburbs of Wilhelmsburg, Altona, and Wandsbek to the city, which in return has to give other areas up to Prussia.
1943	Allied bombers destroy half the city (24th to 26th July).

1952	Hamburg approves the Constitution which is still in force today.
1974	A new landmark is completed: the Köhlbrandbrücke (the suspension bridge across the docks).
1975	The second tunnel under the Elbe is opened.

A walk through Hamburg's old town centre

This journey of exploration to the historical sights of the Free and Hanseatic City of Hamburg starts and finishes at the **mainline station** ❶. This has the largest free-span roof of any railway station in Germany, 120 x 140 metres and 35 metres high. Under its steel and glass roof is a large number of restaurants, kiosks, and shops, which are particularly popular because they stay open longer in the evenings and the week-ends. To reach the old town centre we leave in the direction of the main street called Steintorwall. From the open space in front of the station we cast a glance back to the massive building, built at the beginning of the 20th century in the Wilhelmine style (the style of the era of Kaiser Wilhelm I and II 1871 - 1918), but altered and extended many times since then. Half-left opposite the station, on the other side of Steintorwall, is the start of **Mönckebergstrasse** ❷, the shopping street with the hig-

hest level of turnover anywhere in Hamburg. Along this street stands one major German department store after another, flanked by renowned specialist shops for young fashions, classic clothing, shoes, clocks and watches, and jewellery. The "Boulevard of Shopping Dreams" takes in a quarter of a million visitors every day, with entertainment from street musicians and peddlers.

The main hall of the Hamburg mainline railway station

After the mainline station was built, the city broke open a passage through the old town centre from the Town Hall to the station and arranged for shops and stores to be built on top of the underground railway, which was built at the same time. A few façades have been preserved from this period around 1910, in the area of Nos. 7 to 11 on the left-hand side. Above the row of houses on the left, a slender tower shows us the way to the city church, **St. Jacob** ❸, near the Mönckebergstrasse underground railway station. It was mainly built in the 14th century, but almost completely destroyed by bombing in 1944. It was given its present-day modern tower when it was rebuilt, which was from 1951 onwards. Inside, the altars have been preserved which are dedicated to St Luke (1499), St Peter (1508), and the Holy Trinity (16th century), as has the stone pulpit (1610). However, the church is most famous for its Schnitger organ (1689- 93), on which Johann Sebastian Bach once played.

Returning to the Mönckeberg-strasse we see a pleasing classical building on the right which was built as a library and is reminiscent of a Doric temple. It is a work of the city architect Fritz Schumacher, who did most of the planning work on the Mönckebergstrasse. The fountain (1913-15) in front of the pillars, designed by Georg Wrba, is also based on his designs. The column, crowned with lions and flanked by bronze statues, includes a portrait of the Lord Mayor of Hamburg, J.G. Mönckeberg (1839-1908) after whom the street and the fountain are named.

On the right, the Mönckeberg-strasse opens up to form the Gerhart Hauptmann Platz, with the complex of the State Bank into which the gallery of the same name is integrated. On the north-western side of the square is the traditional "Thalia" theatre, at which many famous personalities of the German-speaking theatrical world have appeared.

St Jacobi church: the famous Arp Schnitger organ (1693) in the west gallery.

It is only a few yards from here to the central church of **St Peter** ❹, which stands directly on the Mönckebergstrasse. The building in front of it was built in 1910/11 to house various arts and crafts, and is named after the man who built it, G. Hulbe. It was intended as an accentpiece when this main shopping street was being laid out. The medallions and the decorative garlands are part of the rich decoration in the style of the Dutch Renaissance, a style which spread throughout the North Sea cities.

A memorial plaque on the neighbouring church commemorates the theologian and resistance fighter Dietrich Bonnhoeffer, executed by the Nazis in 1945 in the

9

The Mönckeberg fountain in Hamburg's main shopping street

Schlossenburg concentration camp. The church of St Peter is the oldest in the city centre, and is mentioned in records as the "Market church" as long ago as 1195. It was rebuilt some time prior to 1350 as a triple-aisle brick-built church, and enlarged in 1418/19 with a second transept on the southern side. It was almost entirely destroyed in the Great Fire of 1842, but then rebuilt along neo- Gothic lines which emphasised the central character of the interior. The only one of all the artistic treasures originally built into the church which has been preserved is the altar, a work

St Peter's church: the view down the nave to the Choir.

by the famous master craftsman Bertram of Minden. He lived and worked in Hamburg from 1367 to 1410. The "Grabow Altar" escaped the inferno as it had been transferred in 1731 to the church of Grabow; it can now be seen the Museum of Art. Only one of the ancient artistic treasures was salvaged from the ashes and rubble in 1842: a bronze lion's head dating from 1342. It is now once again serving as a door-closer on the main door of the church.

The Mönckebergstrasse is about a kilometre in length, and leads at its far end onto the generously proportioned Rathausmarkt [Town hall market], which presents a view of Hamburg's most famous building, the **Rathaus** ❺.

St Peter's church:
Statute to St Ansgar (about 1480)

The monument to Heinrich Heine has been gracing the square since 1982, when the whole area was redesigned and modernised. An older monument to this Jewish poet had been erected in 1926 but then destroyed by the Nazis, and the metal melted down for use in armaments. The city authorities decided to move the mounted statue of the Emperor Wilhelm I, erected in 1903, to the Sievekingplatz. The two flag poles remained in place in front of the Rathaus, decorated with leaves and floral ornamentation and crowned with two golden sailing ships as a reminder of the glorious past of this seafarers' metropolis. The presentday Rathaus was built in 1886-97 in the neo-Renaissance style as a symbol of the city's self-confidence and as the seat of the Senate and the Bürgerschaft, the city-state's parliament. In 1842 the old town hall, which had stood alongside the Trostbrücke bridge, had been blown up on the orders of the city

Guided tours of the Rathaus: *Mondays to Thursdays, 10 am to 3 pm; Fridays to Sundays, 10 am to 1 pm; every half-hour Guided tours in English and French: Mondays to Thursdays, 10.15 am to 3.15 pm; Fridays to Sundays, 10.15 am to 1.15 pm; every hour.* **No guided tours when official events are taking place.** **Information: telephone 040/42831-2470**

Hamburg's Town Hall, built in 1886-97 in a style copying the Renaissance

authorities during the course of the Great Fire in order to save the houses behind it; and this made the new building necessary.

The large site of the former St John's Monastery, which had originally settled on this site in 1230, was an obvious choice. The building took 11 years to build and cost 11 million Gold Marks. Because of the marshy nature of the site, this massive building stands on 4,000 oak piles.

The 112-metre tower marks the centre of the Rathaus façade with the main entrance. As the structure, which is 112 metres long and 78 metres wide, was only slightly damaged during the war, all the prestige rooms have been preserved in their original state and are of course worth visiting. In total the Rathaus consists of 647 rooms, which is 6 more than Buckingham Palace in London. Passing artistically wrought iron grilles and under the magnificent colours of the coat-of-arms, we enter the central hall where the guided tour starts. The councillors' wine cellar invites us in to rest awhile. Plaques on the massive columns commemorate famous citizens of Hamburg. The two generously proportioned stairways symbolise the essential dichotomy of the building; in the East Wing is the accommodation for the Bürgerschaft, in the West Wing is the Senate.

The expensive materials used in the interior bear witness to the Hanseatic city's economic power; thus the Bürgerschaft staircase is designed in marble, bronze, and brass. The ceiling paintings show

Town hall: Stairs leading up to the Senate wing

Emperor's hall with the monumental fresco of the ceiling "The Triumph of the German Flag".

Entrance hall of the city hall.

candidate, in Bürgerschaft elections. The life of a Hanseatic citizen shown here includes family life, trade, art, and science, a mixture which is to this day a typical feature of the metropolis of Hamburg.

The wall paintings show the building by the Trostbrücke, where the Bürgerschaft met after 1842, and the landing bridges in about 1900. The table in the middle of the room consists of a slice taken from an extremely old oak tree trunk which was found during the building work and had probably served as a supporting pillar in the former St Johns' monastery. Passing the Bürgerschaft Council

the sequence of a Hamburg citizen's life, from the cradle to a grand old age. As a grown-up he has to give the Citizen's Oath, which up to 1918 only those inhabitants were allowed to swear who paid at least 1,200 Gold Marks in tax. This was the qualification for voting, or standing as a

Tower room: Paintings decorate the walls and ceiling

Chamber, the guided tour goes on the Bürgersaal, which is a meeting room for the council members and a reception room for their President. One particular feature is the felt carpets which were steeped in oil and then pressed in order to produce a very hard-wearing material. As in other rooms, the paintings and other works of art here came into the town hall as donations from wealthy merchant families. The wide variety of carpentry in the numerous rooms mainly uses walnut, oak, and mahogany, and the doors are in many cases decorated with artistic inlay work for which brass, mother-of-pearl, and ivory were used. In 1895, only two years after the town hall had been officially opened, the Emperor Wilhelm II stayed in the adjoining room, which since then has been called the Kaisersaal or Emperor's Room. Its walls are elegantly clad with leather hangings, and a bronze plaque commemorates the reason for the royal visit: the opening of the Kiel Canal. Three busts depict well-known statesmen of the time when the canal was built: von Moltke, Bismarck, and the Emperor Wilhelm I, the grandfather of Wilhelm II (who was the last German "Kaiser"). Paintings of former Lord Mayors decorate the room, which is sometimes used nowadays by the Senate and the Bürgerschaft for official dinners.

The next room is a tower room mainly used for the traditional New Year's Reception in honour of the Lord Mayor, to which every citizen is most welcome. In addition to a bust depicting Friedrich Ebert, the first President of Germany after the abolition of the monarchy in 1918, and Theodor Heuss, the first Federal President after the second world war, one's

Amsterdam.

In the Lord Mayor's room, which is used today for Senate receptions, the leather wall-hangings are even gilded. Busts of former Lord Mayors bear witness to the tradition of this room, but this applies even more strongly to the wall painting which depicts the entire Senate of 1897 attending the dedication of the building. In compli-

Plenary assembly hall of the City Parliament. The City Parliament consists of 121 members who are elected for 4 years.

attention is primarily caught by the eight valuable columns. They originated from Marocco and are made of the semi-precious stone onyx. Paintings represent the four oldest city-republics in Europe: Athens, Rome, Venice, and

ance with the regulations in force up to 1918, they wore "Spanish merchant's dress", which weighed some 35 kilos.

The Waisenzimmer or orphans' room takes its name from the 80 orphan boys who decorated the

Mayor's hall

Major's office

The Senate's session hall, called "Ratsstube" (council room)

room, with its ceiling, wainscoting, and picture frames with wood-carving work - a project of meticulous work which lasted five years. Another remarkable sight is the chairs, decorated with inlay work, which found their way into the Rathaus as a gift from the neighbouring towns. In the Senate Wing the tour also includes the gracefully decorated Phoenix room, the Ratsstube or councillors' room, and finally the staircase.

commemorate the cholera epidemic of 1892, which cost 8,600 lives and wakened everybody to the urgent need for proper drinking water.

The Hamburg stock exchange was the first one in Germany, having been founded in 1558. Trading initially took place in the open air before being transferred to a building. Part of the present structure, in the classical style, dates from before the Great Fire of 1842, and was extended during the course of

View through the Alster arcades to the town hall tower.

Crossing the entrance vestibule the visitor arrives in the internal courtyard, which is formed by the three wings of the Rathaus and the Hamburg stock exchange. In the centre is the Hygieia fountain (1895 / 96); the goddess of health was given this place of honour to

the 19th century until it reached its present size. Still today the stock quotation board reminds of the activities of the Hanseatic Stock Exchange which was closed on 1st January 2003. For tourist groups it is possible to organise guided tours booking under

View by night across the Binnenalster and the old town centre of Hamburg

with the striking town hall tower and the spires of the Pfarrkirchen

21

Ships' moorings on the Binnenalster.

040/36138-643.

Passing along the main façade of the stock exchange, on Adolphsplatz, we reach the bridge of the same name by the Alsterfleet. This was built on the opposite side from 1842 onwards, together with the rather tropical-looking **Alsterarkaden** ❻. Behind the neo-Renaissance style archway we are attracted by interesting shops and a café. It is very pleasant to sit here in the summer weather and enjoy the magnificent view of the Rathaus across the Kleine Alster with its swans. There is a little architectural jewel here: the Mellin-Passage, which connects the Alsterfleet with the Neuer Wall. The Alster arcades lead along to one of Hamburg's most famous streets, the Jungfernstieg,

which is the border between the Kleine Alster and the lake-like expanse of the Binnenalster. This street is world famous as a mile of boulevard for browsing along and shopping, and contains the prime addresses in Hamburg's business world: jewellers, fashion houses, and also a renowned cinema and a well-known prestige restaurant. On the opposite side, next to the water, there is a traditional café with a breath-taking view, the Alsterpavillon. Immediately next to it there are the moorings for the Alster boats, on which one can make romantic trips across the Aussenalster and even as far as the Elbe by day and in the evening. The bridge opposite is the Lombardsbrücke of 1868, and parallel to it is the modern

Hamburg's latest shopping arcade, the Bleichenhof.

Gänsemarkt-Passage: shopping under a sky made of glass in Hamburg's kilometrelong arcades.

Kennedybrücke; they form the dividing line between the Binnenalster and the Aussenalster. Opposite the Alsterpavillon is a street, Grosse Bleichen, which leads back towards the city centre. This is the start of all the extensive shopping arcades, including the traditional Hamburger Hof and, beyond Poststrasse on the left, the charming Alte Post with its highly up-to-date post-modern Galleria.

Opposite, Hamburg's largest shopping arcade, the colossal Hanse-Viertel, spreads away, linking up to the north with the Gerhofpassage and continuing into other arcades, the Neuer Gänsemarkt and the Gänsemarkt itself. No city in Europe can offer so many roofed-in shopping streets as Hamburg; even in bad weather one can wander for hours dry-shod and enjoy the window-shopping. In Grosse Bleichen there is also the plain façade of a theatre, the Ohnsorgtheater, which many people have seen on television. However, visitors should bear in mind that the popular plays are presented here in plattdeutsch or Low German, the dialect of the northern coast, and not in the virtually High German language of the televised performances. On the left, the series of roofed-in shopping streets continues with the Kaufmannshaus, a cool structure of glass and steel, and the Bleichenhof, Hamburg's youngest arcade, all contributing to making shopping in the Hanseatic city a pure pleasure. Grosser Bleichen ends at Axel

Beautiful view of the Aussenalster and the Binnenalster, divided by the Kennedy and Lombard bridges.

In the background: the Elbe with the port facilities and the docks.

Springer Platz. We will keep over to the left and then turn off right into Düsternstrasse, which then continues as Herrengraben. We pass the Stadthausbrücke underground railway station, noting it as a good starting point for a delightful evening stroll because, to the west of this, in the middle of the former Gängeviertel, there is a centre of stylish entertainment for the more mature kind of youngster. The square develops a particular atmosphere of its own when, on warm summer evenings, the tables and benches can stand in the open air and the guests from the neighbouring wine bars and beer pubs merge together into one enormous mass. However, we will continue on our way along the Herrengraben, and save the pub-crawl until the evening. On the other side of the busy Ludwig Erhard Strasse we can cross Martin Luther Strasse and another street called Teilfeld to reach Krayenkamp, where the **Krameramtswohnungen** ❼ , alms houses, have been preserved in the

The Krameramtswohnungen are alms houses built in 1676 for the widows of small traders.

immediate vicinity of the "Michel". At No. 10 there is the entrance to a long passage framed by close-huddled half-timbered cottages. These were a donation made by the Krameramt, an early form of trade supervisory office, in 1676 for the impoverished widows of small traders

---

ⓘ *Information*

Visiting hours of the church and the tower (lift): *Nov. to March, Mon. to Sat. 10 am to 5 pm, Sun. 11 am to 5 pm; April to Oct., Mon. to Sat. 9 am to 6 pm, Sun. 11 am to 5.30 pm. During services it is not possible to visit the church.* ***Crypt with exhibition "Michaelitica":*** *Nov. to March every day except Tues. and Thurs. 11 am to 4.30 pm; April to Oct. every day 11 am to 4.30 pm, reservations of guided tours under 040/37678-132.* ***Hamburg History, multivision show on 1000 years of Hamburg history:*** *Mon. to Sat. from 12.30 am every 30 min. till 3.30 pm, Sun. from 11.30 am, during winter months only Thurs., Sat. and Sun.* ***Krameramtswohnungen:*** *Tues. to Sun., 10 am to 5 pm; phone 37501988*

The tower of the "Michel" (132m), the hall-mark of Hamburg.

(Kramer); today they are the last continuous row of Hamburg houses dating from that time. The houses are lettered, not numbered, and form a workshop which is an adjunct of the Museum for Local Hamburg History. Up to 1550 there would only have been a few brick-built huts here, surrounded by fields and gardens. Then a small settlement grew up, and the city laid out two cemeteries for the densely populated town area. A chapel of prayer was then built in 1600 near the site of the present **St Michael's Church** ❽ , but it needed expanding only two year's later. Finally in 1606, the city dedicated a further extension, and this became the first " Michaeliskirche" - which we will refer to here by its true Hamburg name of "Michel". At the outbreak of the Thirty Years' War a massive fortified wall incorporated this area as a new part of the town into the defensive ring around Hamburg. The population then grew rapidly, mainly because of refugees flooding in from the surrounding countryside. A larger church was thus soon needed, and the first large "Michel" was consecrated in 1661, and drew praise on account of its beauty as the true hall-mark of the city. It was not until 1747 that the smaller church was pulled down, having become only fit for demolition, but only three years later its larger sister was reduced to rubble after having been struck by lightning. This led to the construction of an entirely new church under two architects: Prey, who only lived to see the start of construction work, and Ernst Georg Sonnin. Sonnin's plan formed the basis of the church as it stands today, and this church was completed in 1762. The 132-metre tall tower was added in 1786; it harmonises beautifully, and can be seen from far away down-river. Although Hamburg's most greatly loved church was completely destroyed by fire in 1906, the city had it rebuilt to Sonnin's plans. Even the serious damage caused by air raids in 1944 and 1945 has long since been repaired. As the hall-mark of the city it at the same time also symbolises its powers of survival. The richly decorated tower portal forms the main entrance to the church. Hamburg is depicted as being under the protection of Heaven in the stainedglass window over the carving work of the doors. The 4.60-metre tall figure of the patron saint, St Michael, above the keystone, is shown defeating the elements of evil, embodied in the shape of Satan, under the sign of the Cross. A memorial plaque in the tower porch commemorates the crew of the training ship Admiral Karpfanger, which sank in 1938. The present-day "Michel" is the third large church on the site, but it still stands on the 1762 foundation walls and is held up by only four massive pillars. With a length of 71 metres and a width of 51 metres, it can seat 2,550 people.

The Altar of the "Michel" with its huge glass mosaic triptych.

The decoration mainly dates from the beginning of this century, and represents worthy craftsmanship in all kinds of precious materials: the lower pews and the doors are made of teak, the carved coats-of-arms on the pews for the Senate and the Dean and Chapter, the 20-metre long altar made of marble with the glass mosaic and the bas-relief of the Last Supper made of gilded bronze, as well as the marble pulpit with its richly decorated acoustic roof reaching out far into the interior. The font was made out of white marble in Livorno, in 1763, and Hamburg merchants then bought it for their church. The same year saw the creation of the wrought iron collection box on the south-west pillar (Hamburg people happily call it the "God-

The enormous interior of the "Michel", with the great organ and the shiplike pulpit in front of the High Altar.

box"), and the first major organ in the church, which attained world-wide fame on account of its dimensions and its sound. After it had been destroyed in the 1906 fire, the congregation was presented with the largest church organ in the world - 163 registers,

of this church. He is buried in the crypt below the church alongside Carl Philipp Emannuel Bach and other famous people, and in the crypt there is also an exhibition showing the history of the church. In clear weather, the top of the tower is highly recommended.

The crypt of the "Michel" contains the tombstones of many famous Hamburg people.

12,173 pipes - by the Godeffroy family foundation. This master-piece was in turn destroyed, by warfare in 1945, and the present-day organ (with 85 registers and 6,665 pipes) took its place in 1962; however, a commemorative plaque on the balustrade of the central gallery still reminds us of this majestic musical instrument. The attraction of the vestry, on the south side of the choir, is its rich-ly carved doors, a fine baroque stucco ceiling, and the pleasing altar. Behind the pulpit, on the south side of the altar, is a portrait of Ernst Georg Sonnin, the builder

The highest platform is almost 83 metres above the ground; by taking the lift you can miss out the 449 steps. The walls are 6 metres thick at the base; their molten inner faces indicate the intensity of the 1906 fire. From the top, the visitor has a magnificent view all across the old town centre and the modern suburbs of Hamburg, and right across the docklands and the Elbe. A bugler used to sound the hours from up here in earlier cen-turies, and in memory of this a chorale is sounded every working day, at 10.00 am and 9.00 pm, and on Sundays at 12.00, to all four points of the compass. Only a few metres below this top platform is Germany's largest tower mounted clock. Until 1964 it was controlled by a pendulum mechanism with a weight weighing 19 hundredweight; nowadays this has been replaced by an electric motor. The face of the clock is 8 metres in diameter, and the hands weigh 130 kilos; the big hand is 4.91 metres long, the little one 3.65 metres, and the big hand moves 40 cm forwards every minute. The largest of the bronze bells is 1.96 metres in diameter and weighs all of 4.9 metric tonnes. When leaving the "Michel" we can cast a glance at the fine Luther memorial on the north side of the tower. This will bring us back in the direction of Ludwig Erhard Strasse, which we can follow to the left until we reach the Alter Elbepark. On the hill in the middle of this park stands the 34-metre colossus of the first German Reichskanzler [Chancellor of the German Empire], Prince Otto von Bismarck (1815 - 98). A committee of Hamburg citizens, plus the Senate and the Bürgerschaft of the Hanseatic city, had the **Bismarck memorial** ❾ erected at this highly visible point in 1903 - 06; it can even be seen from the river near the landing bridges. The main figure is carved from granite, and is reminiscent of medieval

statues of the legendary hero Roland. It is meant to symbolise both the protective hand of the German Empire over seafarers and overseas trade as well as the Imperial claim of the day that Hamburg was "the Gateway to the World". The next major crossroads is at Millerntorplatz, and here we turn off down to the right along Holstenwall. On its left is a park, the Grosse Wallanlage ["main fortifications"], which has pleasant footpaths and extensive stretches of water. The fortifications have long since disappeared, and the Museum of **Hamburg History** ❿ now stands here. The building was designed by the

Model ship: "Wappen von Hamburg".

Museum of Hamburg History:
Tuesdays to Saturday 10 am to 5 pm. Sunday 10 am to 6 pm
Telephone 040/428132-2380.

town architect Fritz Schumacher, and its façade contains elements from some of the city's historical buildings. The exhibition is most interesting, and presents models and objects from the city and its docks in a display area of 7,000

zens' houses have been reconstructed here with the same attention to detail as in Neanderstrasse, which leads off it at an angle. The baroque monastery Beylingstift (1751), at Peterstrasse 35-39, contains the Johannes Brahms Mu-

The Johannes Brahms Museum in Peterstrasse.

square metres. This covers all stages of the city's development, including an illustration of the original Reeperbahn - today the centre of live entertainment, but the name actually means a rope-walk, and the exhibition shows ropemakers at work producing ropes and hawsers. Other particular points of attraction are the model railway, which reproduces the tracks between Hamburg and Harburg on an area of 250 square metres, the model of the docks, and an authentic reproduction of a Hamburg merchant's house of the 17th century. Diagonally opposite, Peterstrasse leads off Holstenwall. Old Hamburg citi-

seum. Returning to the Millerntorplatz, the Ludwig Erhard Strasse continues in the form of the **Reeperbahn** ⓫, probably Germany's most famous street. This is the centre of Hamburg's night-life, where "night is turned into day", if only because the police do not impose any closing hours here. On the right-hand side of the street is the "Café Keese", famous for its "paradox ball" - dancing in which it is the ladies who choose the partners, and where there is a telephone on each table. On the left the row of houses starts with the operetta theatre in which successful musicals have been running for years. The next

Night turns into day: the Reeperbahn knows no closing hours by the police.

is the "Panoptikum", a wax-works showing more than 100 famous personalities, and then "Schmidt & Schmidt's Tivoli", a collection of small theatres for cabaret, music, puppets and marionettes, and variety acts. The St-Pauli-Theater is 150 years old and presents folk-art plays, and the next building is Hamburg's most famous police station, the Davidswache. All along the "Mile of Sin" are bars and taverns of all shapes and sizes, sex cinemas and peep-shows, and in fact everything that any decent red-light district ought to be able to offer. In addition to this, Hamburg's younger generation, including those who have stayed young while growing older, have discovered the delights and unconventional qualities of this district, and now bars, dance-halls, and live music clubs have established themselves here by the dozen. They include Bavarian oompah-music, South American rhythms, sea-shanties, discos with rock and techno-music, cosy meeting-places for artists and the highly authentic Soviet bar, the Gorki Park, not to mention gambling arcades, horserace betting shops, and erotic performances. A charming combination of casual living, culture, and merry night-life has developed here alongside theatres, museums, and art galleries. The main sex shows are concentrated in Grosse Freiheit, a sidestreet that leads off the Reeperbahn to the right in which the traditional atmosphere of the "Mile of Sin" has been preserved although, on the other hand, it was in this street that The Beatles once started their world career. A

WHEN NIGHT FALLS ON ST. PAULI ...

museum was recently opened in No. 7 dedicated to a much-loved Hamburg actor, Hans Albers. Anyone who is around here in daylight hours should turn off at the Davidswache and head towards the Elbe, following the Davidstrasse, which is unmistakably part of the entertainment district. It intersects the notorious Herbert Strasse, to which only men are normally admitted - otherwise there may be trouble from the "ladies" sitting in the windows. On the other hand, female company is very welcome in the Erotic Art Museum, which is to be found a little nearer the docks at Bernhard Nocht Strasse 69. This remarkable collection shows more than 500 paintings, drawings, and statues drawn from the field of erotic art. The Davidstreppe (a flight of steps) takes us down to the Hafenstrasse,

which likewise achieved television fame when squatters resisted eviction when the rightful owners attempted to modernise the houses. The fact that some of the houses have still not yet been emptied is a token of the liberal attitude of the Hamburg city council. We will keep to the left, and this will bring us straight up to a domed, sandstone building erected in 1907 - 09 as the entrance the old Elbe tunnel. From here a lift shaft leads down 23.5 metres to the start of the tunnel, which is 426 metres long, passes 12 metres under the bed of the Elbe, and comes out in the suburb of Steinwerder. In addition to the pedestrian lift there are lifts for raising and lowering two cars at a time. All along the Elbe runs the long sandstone building of the **St Pauli landing bridges** ⓬ . Together with the Elbe tunnel entrance and the den-

St Pauli landing bridges with their distinctive tower.

The famous boat-tours of the docks start from the landing bridges as well.

sely packed buildings above the river, such as the Astra brewery and the Bismarck memorial, this forms Hamburg's welcoming architecture, all typical of the Wilhelmine period. Between Bridges 4 and 5, on the premises of the Tourist Information Department, is the only historical "emigrants' office" in Germany. Its archives contain details of all the emigrants who left between 1850 and 1934, listed by date of departure and by name. For a fee, the office staff can provide information on a total of some five million emigrants. It is from these landing bridges that most of the tourist ships depart on their tours of the docks, which are virtually compulsory for every visitor and are offered in every possible variation: with and without food and drink, music, or dancing. An initial impression of the extensive port

facilities can be gained from the fullcolour model in front of Bridge 1, showing the "world port" as it is today, at the latest stage in a process of development which started in 832. That was when first artificial mooring was created, next to the Hammaburg in the Reichsstrassenfleet, a waterway which has now been filled in. In 1189 the Emperor Friedrich Barbarossa initiated the development of Hamburg into a major overseas port by handing the Hamburg citizens letters patent granting them freedom from taxes and duties all the way down the lower Elbe. Doubt has recently been cast on the authenticity of the signature, as the elderly Emperor set off on a crusade in that same year from which he was never to return. Nevertheless this document, dated 7th May 1189, remained in legal force until

Hamburg was integrated into the German Empire in 1888. As a result of its inherited privileges it succeeded, even at that early stage, in gaining its Free Port Zone, which is still in effect today. Thus the date on Barbarossa's letters patent is still today commemorated as the foundation of the port, and is grandly celebrated every year with all the fun of the fair as the "Harbour's Birthday". In the 12th century, however, the port was located in the Nikolaifleet, where only a few ships could moor. The constant extension of the canals and the moorings continued, and the distance of 120 kilometres from the open waters of the North Sea proved very useful; although the rise of the tide is only two or three metres, it cannot seriously endanger the ships lying in the port. Another advantage to the development of the port was the presence

A view across the Elbe and the port facilities with the innumerable cranes, seen between the towers of the "Michel" and St Katharine's,

of islands in the river, which were integrated into the overall plan. It was because the marshy land was unable to bear any great loads that for instance the present-day Speicherstadt ["warehouse city"], like the Rathaus, was built on thousands of oak piles. These have never needed replacing to this day. 286 ships totalling 52,000 net registered tonnes were sailing under the Hamburg flag in 1850, and by 1910 it was 1,300 ships with a total of over 1.6 million tonnes; Hamburg could indeed proudly proclaim itself to be the "Gateway to the World". This break-neck development pace had been encouraged from 1864 on by how extensive the whole port is. The museum ship Rickmer Rickmers is moored here, a stately three-master of 97 metres length and 3,500 square metres of sail. She was built in 1896 at the Rickmers yard in

...with the ruined tower of the old St Nicholas' church in the background.

◀ *The windjammer "Rickmer Rickmers" once sailed the oceans of the world.*

The classic mixed-cargo freighter "Cap San Diego" is museum ship ▼ today.

Bremerhaven with a steel hull, and sailed many times around Africa to eastern Asia in the years that followed. She was confiscated during the first world war and converted for use by Portugal as a training ship for naval recruits. Later she was equipped with diesel engines, and taken out of service in the official in charge of waterways construction, Dalmann, who turned Hamburg into a major modern port in which the largest ocean-going vessels could dock. Shipping line owners and merchants had made the invaluable contribution of their entrepreneurial spirit and organisational ability. The port facilities today cover an area of 87 square kilometres, with 70 basins available to inland waterway and high seas vessels. It is thus only possible to see from an aeroplane, or by looking at the model, 1962. In 1983 an association called "Windjam-

Information

"Rickmer Rickmers" museum ship:
Every day, 10 am to 6 pm, telephone 0 40/3 19 59 59
"Cap San Diego" museum ship:
Every day, 10 am to 6 pm, telephone 0 40/36 42 09

mers for Hamburg" succeeded in acquiring her, and following thorough restoration she has been moored at the Fiete-Schmidt jetty since 1987 as a seafarers' memorial and museum, showing the visitor the romance of seafaring and also the prime means of locomotion: wind, steam, and diesel. Leaving the St Pauli landing bridges we remain on the Elbe embankment, with the port area stretching away on our right. Another museum ship is moored at Überseebrücke, the Cap San Diego. She was built in a Hamburg yard called simply Deutsche Werft, in 1962, and carried conventional mixed-freight cargoes for the Hamburg-Süd line on a regular service between Europe and the east coast of South America. Überseebrücke, originally the landing stage for the ocean-going liners, can be reached from the part of the embankment road called Vorsetzen, from where tours of the harbour also start. A former fire-fighting vessel is moored to the quay, waiting for customers; it has been converted into a highly original café, restaurant, and pub. Vorsetzen, between the lower harbour on the right and the old Hamburg underground railway (built from 1906 onwards,

Ocean-going vessel in dock at the "Blohm und Voss" yard

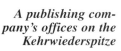

A publishing company's offices on the Kehrwiederspitze

The centre of Hamburg seen from the air: above the Elbe is the "new town" and the "Michel", on the right is the "old town" and the

town hall, and beyond that the Binnenalster and the Aussenalster.

47

and running here well above ground), is continued in the form of Baumwall, the end of which is marked by a bridge, the Nieder-baumbrücke. This connects the quay zone with the Kehrwieder-spitze, which consists mainly of an artificial island formed by the digging of the canals and the inner port. We remain on the edge of the port and pass the Haus der Seefahrt [Seafaring House], the corner building alongside a filled-in Fleet. It was built in 1909 / 10 as a rent-office building. Behind its representative façade with its art nouveau ornamentation is a pillar construction with a staircase and lifts. The floors can thus be divided up in any way required. Merchants' houses typical of the

Facades in Deichstrasse.

Hamburg of the 17th to the 19th century can be seen in the nearby **Deichstrasse** ⓭ , where one of the few complete rows of houses can be seen that came through the Great Fire of 1842, the modernisation of the city, and the air raids of the second world war almost unharmed. Fine brick and baroque façades end in stepped and vaulted gables. The houses most worth looking at are No. 47 (about 1658, with the baroque gateway taken from No. 29 when it was pulled down), and No. 37 (1686). The latter is the sole surviving example of a ceiling passing through two storeys such as was usual in Hamburg patrician houses in the 16th to the 18th century. No. 27 was built in 1780 as a warehouse known as the Bardowik warehouse; its neighbour has a very presentable baroque doorway. Between No. 23 and No. 21 a small passageway runs down to the Fleet from where there is a view along the Nikolaifleet and the rear sides of the houses, some of them in their original halftimbered construction, and many of them with goods doors and blockand- tackle directly over the water. Along the further length of the canal, the old St Nicholas' church makes a charming picture. This Nikolaifleet played a very special role compared with all the many other canals in Hamburg; in the Middle Ages it was the port, and the other Fleete were waterways, drains, the source of water for washing and drinking, and brewing water for most

View across the Nikolaifleet to the romantic merchants' houses in Deichstrasse.

of the renowned brewery companies in Hamburg. The city paid for watchmen, called Fleetkieker, to ensure no dead animals, bricks or stones, or manure was thrown into the canals, as this would principally have been a hazard to shipping; the health of the inhabitants could not always keep up with this state of affairs, and a horrifying cholera epidemic wiped out 8,600 of them in 1892. The next part of Deichstrasse was largely destroyed in 1842. A magnificent example of successful new architecture, put up immediately after the Great Fire, is No. 19, the façade of which boasts rich stucco elements in various historical styles; it is a fine example of romantic histori-

cism. A pedestrian bridge crosses the busy Ost-West Strasse at this point, and brings us to the historic Hopfenmarkt [hop market]. The fountain here, the Vierländerin-brunnen, of 1878, commemorates the Vierländer, the farmers (or in this case a farmer's wife) a little further up the Elbe who have always been Hamburg's main suppliers of fruit and vegetables. The term Vierlande actually covers a fertile stretch of river marshes and consisting of four old parishes owned for centuries by Hamburg and Lübeck jointly until it was annexed to Hamburg in 1867 as the manor of Bergedorf. An inscription re-iterates the old saying: "The market teaches you about people". An information centre displays pictures and documents showing the old **St Nicholas' church**  prior to its destruction. The ruins of it, with its towering spire - with 145 metres it was once the third tallest in Germany - have been left exactly as they were after the bombing of the second world war, to act nowadays as a call to peace and a monument to the 50,000 people who died in the air raids in Hamburg alone. After passing the ruin, we leave the Ost-West Strasse and cross the Nikolaifleet by the Trostbrücke; this was the port of Hamburg in the Middle Ages, and at the same time formed the dividing line between the "old" and the "new" town. The two statues depict Archbishop Ansgar, who made "Hammaburg" his see in the 9th century, and Count Adolf II of Schauenburg, the founder of the new town. We will keep to the right, along "Bei der Alten Börse", which runs up to Hamburg's oldest bridge, the Zollenbrücke (1633). Its name means "customs bridge" and comes from the former customs house; it was rebuilt fully authentically in 1955. From the Gröningerstrassefleet, which it spans, only a small residue remains; most of the Fleete in the city have been completely filled in. Following the line of the

▲ *Statue to St Ansgar on the Trostbrücke.*
▼ *The Trostbrücke spans the Nikolaifleet.*

View from the Speicherstadt across Zollkanal to St Katharine's church.

51

Zollenbrücke we cross Ost-West Strasse and then use the tower of **St Katharine's Church**  as a guide. There was an earlier church on this site as long ago as the 13th century. The present-day three-nave church was built in the 14th and 15th centuries in the brick Gothic style; the baroque dome on the tower and the west front are of a later date. Valuable tombstones have been preserved from the late Renaissance period such as the epitaphs of Lord Mayor Wetken, dedicated in 1566 to his sons, who had died young, and of Councillor Moller, who died in 1610. These are made of sandstone, marble, and alabaster; the next tombstone is of Councillor von der Fechte, who died in 1630. On the other hand, only two works of art have been preserved from pre-war times, the corpus (about 1300) of the crucifix in the southern aisle, and a statue of St Katharine, southern German work of the 15th century. The most noteworthy of the later additions are the three glass pictures (1955 - 57) and the bronze door in the south doorway, and the memorial to the 80 victims of the loss of the training schooner Pamir in 1957. As long ago as the 17th century there was a bridge linking St Katharine's churchyard with the island opposite, Brookinsel, which, like the Kehrwieder district to the right of it was densely populated and provided low-cost housing for dock workers, who thus did not have far to walk. During the course of time

St Katharine, statue (15th century) in the church of the same name.

numerous merchants settled there as well, but this process of structural change accelerated rapidly from 1888 onwards; in less than a quarter of a century there arose the **Speicherstadt** , or "city of warehouses", now the biggest in the world, with (for those days) ultramodern office and storage buildings which can be approached from the water and from the land side. There was a price to be paid, and it was of course the "little man" who paid it; more than 18,000 inhabitants had to leave their homes to make room for a modernisation programme which was, in its day, revolutionary. They were rehoused in such suburbs as Winterhude and Barmbek. We can reach the island by cros-

▲ *German Customs Museum in the Speicherstadt. The ship in the canal is the former customs cruiser "Glückstadt".*

◄ *Customs Museum: scales.*

▼ *Customs Museum: smugglers' hide-holes.*

sing the Jungfernbrücke across the Zollkanal. A revolving door at the island end marks the start of the Free Port Zone, to which the Speicherstadt belongs. All goods arriving here are landed customs-free, so even a casual visitor is subject to customs regulations. If we follow the street called Neuer Wandrahm it will lead us on to the

German Customs Museum:
Tuesdays to Sundays, 10 am to 5 pm, phone 300876-11
Free entrance. Guided tours on request (by telephone).

next street, Alter Wandrahm. No. 15a, the former Kornhausbrücke customs office, is the home of the German Customs Museum, where the visitor has an impressive display of the living history of customs and excise, of the work of the individual customs officer yesterday and today, interesting hide-holes used by smugglers, and the old customs cruiser Glückstadt. Returning to the Jungfernbrücke, we now cross Neuer Wandrahm and admire the remarkable brick architecture of the warehouses. The name of one of the streets here, Pickhuben, refers to the Pechhauben, hoods soaked in pitch, which used to be pulled over the heads of criminals being taken for execution on Grosser Grasbrook. Many of them had been pirates, such as the notorious Klaus Störtebeker, who was beheaded here in 1400. In the surroundings you can find the "Hamburg Dungeon", dedicated to the shady side of former times. On a surface of 2200 square metres all details of the gruesome dungeon atmosphere are displayed with horrifying effects. The special highlights are the professional actors who make history real thanks to their convincing representation and superb irony. The time travel starts in an old-fashioned, wobbly lift. After surviving

Hamburg Dungeon, at 2, Kehrwieder (Speicherstadt):
every day 11 am to 6 pm (last entrance). July-August 10
am to 6 pm. Info at 040-36005500 or
www.hamburgdungeon.com

this daredevil tour you can experience the horrors of plague, Inquisition and torture as well as the Great Fire of 1842 and the execution of Störtebeker. Visitors can actively take part in this horrific event.

the details which are similar to the original. The fascination of the most successful exhibition in North Germany are the numerous small details and stories which were inserted into the magic miniature landscape by the 120 "crea-

Close to it we can find the next tourist attraction. The **Miniatur Wunderland** is well-known thanks to more than 100 TV-reports. Already more than 2,5 million tourists have been visiting the biggest miniature railway in the world. 370.000 working hours were needed above all for the construction of the whole area and for

tors" of the Miniatur Wunderland. The exhibition attracts the visitor and makes him spend some hours in a very good mood. 34 computers control the plant with its 700 trains, 130.000 lights and remote-controlled cars. More than 100.000 figurines contribute to make this experience unforgettable for the whole family. We,

Miniatur Wunderland, at Kehrwieder 2 (Speicherstadt): every day 9.30 am to 6 pm, Tuesdays 9.30 am to 9 pm, Saturdays, Sundays and public holidays 8.30 am to 8 pm. Phone 040/3006800. www.miniatur-wunderland.de

View from the air of the Speicherstadt and the new "City Port". Since 2003, the Speicherstadt has lost its Free Trade status so that it is possible to access the future, modern City Port direct from the Old City.

 InfoCenter of City Port, at Am Sandtorkai 30, Kesselhaus: *Tuesdays to Sundays 10 am to 6 pm, Thursdays till 9 pm. Phone 040/36901799.*

The storage buildings in the Speicherstadt could be approached from the rear by barges and from the front by horse-drawn or railway wagons.

however, will follow the St-Annen Ufer to the left, then the Holländischer Brook and Dienerreihe to the right. The lively coming-and-going on working days shows that the warehouses, with their enormous storage capacity, are still attractive today although the cranes and railway sidings have long ago given way to the lorry. Here in Hamburg, in

Information

Spicy Museum, at 32, Sandtorkai:
Tuesdays to Sundays, 10 am to 5 pm, phone 367989.
www.spicys.de

The HighFlyer rises to the sky above Hamburg and if it is nice weather it offers a panoramic view well beyond the limits of the town.

any case, there are more oriental carpets in store than in any port in the world, and not one of these warehouses is standing empty. The consequences of aerial warfare are only visible on those few buildings which had to be replaced completely, as a large part of the structural substance was either preserved or has been rebuilt. At Sandtorkai since 1993 there is the Spicy Museum where visitors can smell, touch or taste more than 50 spices. About 800 exhibits from 5 centuries show the cultivation of spices from growing to the finished product. The Museum is housed in a former old warehouse, where you can completely experience the world of spices. At Brooktorkai we leave the Free Port Zone at the customs office and by crossing the Oberbaumbrücke leave the totally unique Speicherstadt. On the right is the site of the former wholesale market, which was moved out to new quarters in the Hammerbrook district in 1962. The two main halls (built from 1900 onwards) have now been restored and are used for major international art exhibitions. Since some years the **"HighFlyer Hamburg"** starts its flight from here. The captive balloon, being 150 metres high, represents the town's highest panorama point. The balloon "takes off" to the sky above Hamburg close to Deichtor halls and if it is nice weather it offers a view of more than 40 kilometres, beyond the limits of the town. The position next to Deichtor halls, at the boundary between city port and old town, gives a view of the new district, of the port and of the town centre with Binnenalster and Aussenalster. With a good visibility it is possible to see all sights and towers of the Hanseatic city of Hamburg. In the basket there is

HighFlyer Hamburg: October to March 10am to 10 pm, April to September 10 am to 12 pm. As flight and shop times depend on the weather it is not possible to book in advance. Hotline: 040/30086969, www.highflyer-hamburg.de

*Original architecture
in the business
district: Chilehaus.*

room for up to 30 persons; more-over the balloon is piloted only by pilots with corresponding licence and training.

After crossing Deichtorplatz, we keep over to the left, heading towards the old town centre, and a few yards further find an architecturally most original building in front of us: **Chilehaus** ⓱ . This is a gigantic brick building divided vertically, the eastern tip of which is designed in the shape of a ship's bow. It was built in 1922 - 24 to the commission of a merchant called Henry Sloman, who mainly traded in saltpetre from Chile, by

the architect Höger, and also inspired the brick face and decorations of the massive neighbouring Sprinkenhof (1928 - 43), which likewise belongs to the business district, as doe the Mohlenhof, the Montanhof, and the Ballinhaus. In this part of the old town centre around Burchardtplatz there used to be the Gängeviertel until the beginning of the 19th century; it was here that the cholera epidemic spread like wildfire. From 1912 onwards the old half-timbered houses were pulled down, and the district rebuilt to an entirely new plan with brick-built office blocks. This created another of the city's hallmarks, mainly planned by the architect Fritz Schumacher, who had previously carried out the reconstruction work on the old town centre. Crossing Mohlenhausstrasse and, turning off to the right, Steinstrasse, we leave the old centre as such at the Steintor-wall tunnel and enter the district of St Georg, dis- tinguished by the distant double church tower of the Catholic church of St Mary. To the south-east of the mainline station, on Steintorplatz, there is an impressive building housing the **Museum of Arts and Crafts** ⓲ , opened in 1877. It contains col- lec- tion of international signifi-

Museum of arts and crafts: ivory statue of "Adam and Eve" (Leonhard Kern, about 1650).

Museum of Art and Crafts:
Tuesdays to Sundays, 10 am to 6 pm (or until 9 pm on Thursdays), telephone 428134-2630.

cance showing applied art from all over Europe, and from the Middle Ages to the present day: rich stocks of ceramics in faience and porcelain, goldsmiths' work, bronzes, ivory, furniture of every epoch and style, as well as sculptures, textiles, and musical instruments and an important collection of posters and photographs. One department is dedicated to the art of classical antiquity and Islam, another presents extensive east-Asian collections of bronzes, porcelain, and wood carvings. In

live down its name, which means "churches avenue"). However, there are cosy pubs and artists' workshops scattered amongst the more dubious houses and numerous hotels, and St Georg does also include such palaces of culture as the Museum of Arts and Crafts, the famous theatre "Deutsches Schauspielhaus" (Kirchenallee 39/41), and the **Kunsthalle** ⓭, an art gallery which is in effect the northward extension of the mainline station. The main part of this building was

Tradition and avant-garde work in the Deutsches Schauspielhaus

addition to this, the Museum possesses a famous collection of art nouveau work including the "Paris room", bought up from the World Exhibition of 1900. Constantly changing special exhibitions offer the regular visitor new artistic pleasures. Kirchenallee leads along the eastern side of the mainline station, forming the gateway to the entertainments district of St Georg (as if trying to

put up in 1914-21 as a harmonising extension in the Italian Renaissance style to the older, brick-built structure dating from 1869. The art collection in the interior of this complex of buildings is one of the most significant in any German-speaking country, and one in which special attention has been devoted to the art of recent times. One unique feature is the number of works by

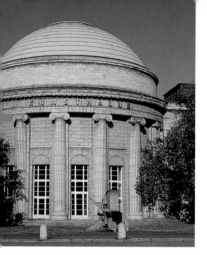

The Hamburg Kunsthalle houses a significant collection of works of art from all the German-speaking countries.

Kunsthalle: "Nana"
(1877, Edouard Manet)

19th century German painters, represented by such well known artists as Caspar David Friedrich, Max Liebermann, Philipp Otto Runge, Adolph von Menzel, and Wilhelm Leibl. Another highpoint is 20th century art, with outstanding groups of works by Nolde, Dix, Beckmann, Kokoschka, Klee, and Picasso. Amongst the older works, the principal ones are medieval altars by such masters as Bertram and Francke, as well as paintings by Rembrandt, Ruisdael, Claude Lorrain, and Boucher. The collection of 19th and 20th century sculptures also deserve attention. We end our tour of Hamburg by returning to the mainline station. However, the sheer size of the city means that we will have had no choice but to ignore many sights worth seeing, so we recommend that you visit some of these by public transport. The city offers a bargain for this: the "Hamburg Card", valid for all local public transport, for free entry into the museums, and a reduced rate for tours round the city, the docks, and the Alster, and for visiting the museum ships.

Hamburg Kunsthalle:
Tuesdays to Sundays, 10.00 am to 6.00 pm (or until 9.00 pm on Thursdays). Telephone 428131200

North of the old town centre

The suburban electric railway (routes 11, 21, and 31) carry us to Dammtor station, which we leave in the direction of Dag Hammarskjöld Platz. In front of us is one of the generously proportioned areas of parks and gardens of this city. It consists of the old botanical garden (on the left) and, beyond it, the city's most famous park, "**Planten un Blomen**" ("plants and flowers", in the dialect), flanked by a hotel sky-scraper and congress centre and the exhibition halls of the Hamburger Messe. Rocks and water, trees and flowers, bushes and shrubs compete for the visitor's favour. The impressive points of attraction are also the tropical house and Europe's biggest Japanese garden, as well as the gigantic water-and-light organ which plays a colourful concert at night-time during the summer months. The modern Congress Centre of Hamburg (CCH) is equipped to meet every need, with a total of 17 conference rooms and auditoria seating 50 to 3,000 peo-

Water playing in the green leisure facility of "Planten un Blomen".

View across "Planten un Blomen" to the television tower from the skyscraper hotel the congress centre.

ple. It is linked to a 32-storey hotel. To the west stands Hamburg's tallest structure, the **television tower**, rising to a grand 280 metres (and known to the locals as "Kuchen-Michel" because the restaurant at the top serves coffee and cake generously.) The visitor can only travel up to a height of 128 metres, but that is sufficient for a fantastic panorama view. Quite near the Hamburger Messe, on the St Pauli side, is the **Heiligengeistfeld** (underground to Feldstrasse station) with the Hochbunker multi-storey air-raid shelter, the ground of Hamburg's second main football team, FC St Pauli, and extensi-

Symphony Orchestra. It is not far from here to the Gänsemarkt underground station, which one can reach by going along Dragonerstall and Valentinskamp. The street called Dammtor branches off to the left here, and in this street stands the Hamburg State **Opera House**. It is one of the most famous theatres in the world, and its ballet is world-famous. If we follow Dammtor, and then Dammtordamm to Theodor Heuss Platz, leaving this northwards along Rothenbaumchausee, we can see the "Moorweide" stretching away to our right; this is a popular open park with sports

Hamburg's Musikhalle at Johannes Brahms Square.

ve parking facilities. Three times a year, for one month at a time, there is a traditional fair here called the "Dom". Along the south side of these parks is the Gorch Fock Wall, where the baroque **Musikhalle** stands, the focal point of Hamburg's rich concert life and frequently the venue for the State Philharmonic Orchestra, the NDR [North German Radio] Symphony Orchestra, and the Hamburg

grounds and lawns, much loved by the Hamburg student population. On its edge is Amerika-Haus, a symbol of the traditional friendship between the two countries. On its left is where the **university district** starts, with the striking, domed main building of Germany's fifth largest university. The Platz der jüdischen Deportierten ["Square of the Jewish Deportees"] commemorates both

Ship's mooring on the Aussenalster.

the time of Nazi racial hatred and the fact that the university building stands on the site of the Jewish quarter, which used to be very extensive. The main shopping street is Grindelallee, with a wide range of restaurants, book-shops, CD shops, and poster shops specially for young people. From Rothenbaumchaussee we can reach the **Hamburg Museum of Ethnology**. Thanks to the city's world-wide trading links and to donations from its citizens, a start was made more than 100 years ago with the construction of this highly valuable collection. It is divided into seven departments, showing about 350,000 exhibits from all parts of the world and almost as many photographs of aboriginal inhabitants. The treasures include the famous "Gold chamber", with gold items from Latin America, bronze castings and ivory carvings from West Africa, the biggest Siberian collection outside Russia, and many unusual treasures from the South Seas.

Further north, Hartungstrasse branches off to the left; this is where the traditional theatre group Neue Kammerspiele resides. In **Rothenbaumchaussee** is the

Museum of Ethnology:
Tuesdays to Sundays, 10 am to 6 pm (or to 9 pm on Thursdays). Telephone 01805-308888

practice ground of Hamburg's first division football team Hamburger Sportverein - universally known as HSV. From the nearby underground station of Hallerstrasse we can reach the extensive, beautiful **Alsterpark** on the banks of the Aussenalster. The landscape is magnificent and makes the surrounding suburbs the finest in Hamburg: Rothenbaum and Harvestehude to the west, and Winterhude, Barmbek-Süd, and Uhlenhorst to the east. The Aussenalster and the Fleete with their magnificent villas and art nouveau façades invite the visitor to take a stroll. Splendid old buildings are also to be found in the next suburb, Eppendorf, which dominated Hamburg night life in the 1970's. Another pleasure is the numerous restaurants, representing the higher levels of the catering trade. Twice a week there is the exclusive Isemarkt, a street market in Isestrasse, underneath the ele-

vated railway, enticing lovers of unconsidered trifles, just as the miles and miles of shopping streets in Eppendorfer Weg and Eppendorfer Landstrasse have their regular customers as well. Only **Pöseldorf**, directly above the Alsterpark, is the odd man out amongst these upper-middle class residential areas. This was once an area of allotments and market gardens, but then smaller traders settled here, as can still easily be seen from the narrow alleys and tiny craftsmen's houses. Nowadays they house fashion boutiques, art galleries, and antique shops, traditional restaurants, and cosy pubs. North of Winterhude and Barmbek-Süd is the **Stadtpark**, many times larger than the Alsterpark. We can reach it from here by underground, changing at Kellinghusenstrasse station from Line U1 to U3 (in the direction of Barmbek). Borgweg station is located right in the middle of the park, which also conceals a **plane-**

Aussenalster: Sailing dinghies in the middle of a big city.

Planetarium in Hamburg's Stadtpark.

tarium. The dome is 21 metres in diameter, making it the largest of its kind in Europe. A few kilometres further north is Hamburg's international airport in the suburb of Fuhlsbüttel. From the centre of Hamburg it takes very little time to reach the famous **Hagenbeck's zoo** by underground (Line U2), in the suburb of Stellingen. This traditional family concern opened for business in 1907, and soon earned world-wide respect because it was the first to be laid out exclusively with open-air paddocks, even for the wildest animals. The magnificent park-like landscape of 25 hectares is nowadays home to more than 2,100 animals in 50 enclosures, aquariums and terrariums, making it one of the biggest zoos in Germany. Entertainment for guests is provided by the Dolphin Show, the exotic "Jungle Nights", and the elephant rides. Between the suburbs of Stellingen and Bahrenfeld there is another large area of parks and gardens - gigantic, by city standards: the main cemetery and the **Volkspark** of Altona, with the Volksparkstadion (the stadium where HSV plays its home matches) and the trotting-race track, where international sporting events are regularly held.

Hagenbeck's zoo: "Let's all go to Hagenbeck!".

To the west of the old town centre

Hamburg's oldest market is the St Pauli **Fischmarkt**, best reached from the landing bridges and along the Elbe. However, it is only open on Sundays, and only until 10 o'clock in the morning! - so it is something for early risers and late-night birds. In the summer it starts at 5.00 am, in the winter at 7.00 am. Near the former fish-auction hall extension of Fischmarkt is first Breite Strasse and then **Palmaille**, once the finest street in the old town centre of **Altona**. Some of the patrician houses have been preserved. The poet Detlef von Lilliencron lived in No. 5, and later No. 100, around the turn of the century. In Max Brauer Allee you can still see the Altona Rathaus of 1896 - 98,

Sunday morning on the Fish Market.

there are all sorts of things on sale: antiques and jumble- sale stuff, vegetables, smoked eel and, almost as an afterthought, fresh-caught fish. In the restored fish-auction hall, visitors with real endurance can order a Jazz Breakfast, assuming he would not prefer to visit one of the original and popular restaurants around the fish market. The further which had once been a railway building. In front of it is an equestrian statue of the Emperor Wilhelm I. Separated from it by the Platz der Republik, and running parallel to Max Brauer Strasse, is Museumstrasse, which to the north passes the Altona Theatre, which took its name from the "**Altona Museum and North German State Museum**",

In front of the imposing façade of the Altona town hall is an equestrian statue of the Emperor Wilhelm I.

one of the biggest regional museums in Germany, dedicated mainly to the cultural history of northern Germany. Among its possessions are 17 original farmhouse room settings, a complete cot tage from the Vierlande region, and a grocery shop complete with furniture, equipment, and traditional costume from the rural area. Other exhibitions are concerned with the subject of seafaring and fishing, and present models of ships and fishing tackle, paintings, figure-heads, nautical instruments, and the working tools of the ship's carpenter and sailmaker. The north German landscape and its inhabitants encounter us again in the art gallery; new collections on the subject of arts and crafts, textiles, toys, and the city history of Altona are being planned. Altona has been a suburb of Hamburg since 1937, but in the 19th century it was, after Copenhagen, the second biggest city in Denmark. The further extension of Museumstrasse brings us to the suburban electric railway station of Altona, from where the No. 183 bus takes us to **Övelgonne Museum**

Altona Museum and North German State Museum:
Tuesdays to Sundays, 11 am to 6 pm.
Telephone 42811-3582

Harbour. Above the (invisible) Elbe tunnel, 20 venerable old ships lie at their moorings. These lovingly restored vessels, such as the luffer Elfriede (this is a one-and-a-half masted coasting vessel) and the retired fire tender Elbe 3, can be visited at any time. The tunnel just referred to, built in 1968 - 75, is just over 3 kilometres long, and thus the longest tunnel under water in the world. A walk through the long drawn-out village of **Övelgonne**, once the home of the river pilots, takes us

museums in the north-west of the park: the **Jenischhaus**, a branch of the Altona Museum, exhibits examples of houses of the better class in the 16th to the 19th century, and the modern **Ernst Barlach house**, dedicated to the work of this famous sculptor and artist (1870 - 1938). The great attraction here is the 23 wood sculptures, which are of the highest artistic value. Baron Voght Strasse, which flanks the park on the west side, takes us (northwards) to Klein Flottbek railway station, and

Venerable old ships in the Övelgonne Museum Harbour.

back into long-forgotten times; lime trees and gas lamps line the embankment road, accompanied on the landward side by idyllic cottages with verandas and decorative wrought iron work, and beautifully tended front gardens.

The bus (no. 36, 39, or 286) which transports us along the **Elbchaussee** soon brings us to the Jenischpark (Teufelsbrück bus-stop), some of which is designated as a nature conservation area. Enchanting park roads lead us to two remarkable

from here it is only two stops to **Blankenese**, once an idyllic fishing village on the Elbe. Here it is worthwhile making a tour with the public mini-bus, route 48, known as the Bergziege [mountain goat]. The view on crooked roads over the hill (5,000 steps!), typical fishermen's cottages with brick façades and thatched roofs, and the magnificent villas on the hills keep making a profound impression. Nowadays this is a "posh" suburb, so it is not surprising that the "mountain goat" only

View of Hamburg's most prestigious suburb, Blankenese.

Ships coming up-river to Hamburg docks are welcomed Willkommhöft

offers First Class seats. From Blankenese station we can most easily reach **Willkommhöft** by taking the bus (route 189). Hamburg's world-famous ship welcoming facility is accommodated in the Schulau ferry house, in the suburb of Wedel. Between dawn and sunset every day, every ship of more than 500 tons is welcomed as it comes up or goes down the river. The appropriate national anthem is played over the loudspeakers, and a few words of welcome addressed to the crew in their own language, whilst the Hamburg flag is dipped. There is also a ship-in-a-bottle museum in the cellar of the ferry house.

Eastwards from the centre

Schloss Ahrensburg

Suburban Electric Line 4 terminates at Ahrensburg, which is outside the city limits and therefore lies in the state of Schleswig-Holstein. We can take the bus to the former moated grange, which is idyllically located slightly outside the town in a magnificent stretch of parkland. It is the enchanting location in particular which made the property frequently suitable as the backdrop for filming. The building itself, with its slender corner turrets, was built in 1595 in the north German Renaissance style, and was based on Schloss Glücksburg, which is barely ten years older. In 1759, Schloss Ahrensburg came into the possession of Count Schimmelmann, who had the reception rooms in particular redesigned in the rococo style, the state in which they can be visited today as a museum. Between the Schloss and

Schloss Ahrensburg: an idyllic moated grange of the Counts Rantzau, in the north German Renaissance style.

the former village of Woldenhorn, which has only taken the name of Ahrenburg since the 19th century, lies the **Schlosskirche**, the church of lords of the grange. The inscriptions over the entrance door record the erection of the church, 1594 - 96, by Count Peter Rantzau. His tombstone was destroyed by the Swedes in 1713, together with the rest of the interior, so the Counts had the church redesigned in 1716 by their court carver, Döbel. Another remarkable feature is the mausoleum of Count Detlef Rantzau, the entrance of which is decorated with an encoded text. To the left there is the year, 1689, and the family coat-of-arms, granted after the elevation of the counts to the rank of Imperial Counts in 1728. Far below are the coats-of-arms of his first and his second wife. The stone sarcophagus in the interior of the chapel is also decorated with names, dates, and coats-of-arms, with the names and dates of birth on the side of his ten children, and conceals the mortal remains of the Count. The successor of the Rantzau line, Count Schimmelmann, had the clock tower built in 1778. The graves of his family are in the old graveyard here around the church. This is flanked in turn, at certain parts, by two rows of interesting oldpeople's houses called the Gottesbuden ["God's rooms"]. Count Peter Rantzau had them built immediately after the church as alms houses, and laid down the amount of the rent: one half Thaler (75 Cent) per month on the south side, no rent payable for the north side.

In the direction of Bergedorf

We now take the local railway Route 2 eastwards, first of all to Bergedorf. Here the original moated castle was changed many times, and extended to make it into a mansion. It is quite near the station, right in the centre of the town, surrounded by parkland which runs as far as the Bille river. Remains of the once high embankments and wide moats of this medieval castle, the only one to be preserved within the limits of the city state, bear witness to its proud military past. The building had been used for a long time as a government offices, but now houses the Museum for Bergedorf and Vierlande with numerous documents and exhibits showing the prehistory and regional history of the area, and the rustic culture of the region as well. From the local electric railway station we can take the 324 bus to the **Rieck Haus open-air museum**, an outside department of the Altona Museum. This is in the suburb of Curslack, one of the four church holdings which gave the "Vierlande" its name. The Rieck Haus is a farmhouse, 450 years old, with a barn, a hayrick, and a windmill. In addition to a remarkable collection of historical items it also possesses a magnificent inlay wall. The suburb of **Neuengamme** adjoins Curslack to the south. It

An outside department of the Altona Museum and North German State Museum: the Rieck Haus (seen from the dike)

attained melancholy fame because, in contrast to the flourishing countryside, the largest concentration camp in the north of Germany stood here from 1938 to the end of the war. There is a memorial on the site now, set up as a plea to avoid human destruction and intolerance, but also a place for understanding and reconciliation. Returning to Bergedorf station, we travel one stop further and visit the third mansion in the area around Hamburg, **Reinbeker Schloss**. It was built in 1576 in the Dutch Renaissance style, an irregular building in three wings with a court of honour and large upper windows. This brick building has been carefully restored and now serves as a cultural centre with exhibitions and concerts.

Reinbeker Schloss (about 1576)

Museum für Bergedorf and the Vierlande: *daily, 11 am to 6 pm, closed on Monday and Friday. Telephone 42891-2509*
Rieck-Haus open-air museum:
Tuesdays to Sundays, 10.00 am to 4.00 pm. Telephone 040/7231223
Neuengamme concentration camp memorial: *Mon. to Fri. 9.30 am to 4 pm, Sat., Sun. and public holidays April to Sept. 12 am to 7 pm; Oct. to March 12 am to 5 pm, phone 428131-500*

Events in Hamburg

The annual calendar of events will soon show that Hamburg people know how to celebrate events and organise festivals. Munich has its Oktoberfest, and Hamburg has its Dom, a gigantic fair on the Heiligengeistfeld in the middle of the city centre, which takes place three times a year for a month at a time and draws huge crowds: in March / April as the Frühlingsdom, from the end of July to the end of August as the Hummelfest or Sommerdom, and the highly traditional Winterdom from early November until well into December. More than 200 showmen outbid one another with attractions and culinary delights. The programme for the "Harbour's birthday" is far more compact. It is celebrated all around the docks for three days, centred on 7th May. In addition to numerous activities on

Huge crowds on the "Harbour's birthday".

Hamburg's most important event, the Dom, takes place three times a year.

dry land there is of course plenty more on the water: regattas, windjammer parades, and fleets to visit, are all on the programme.

Regular features now, and added attractions to the Hanseatic city, are the **historische Automeile** (end of April, in Nedderfeld), the **Stuttgarter Weindorf** (June/July on the Rathausmarkt) and the **Alstervergnügen** (four days at the end of August, all round the Binnenalster). They are supplemented every Sunday by the **Fischmarkt** mentioned above, the **City centre fair** (Mai / June in Mönckebergstrasse), the **Christmas market** which starts in Advent and completely takes over the city centre, and numerous other similar activities in the various suburbs. As a cultural counter-pole there is the **Hamburg Summer** from May to October, with an enormous offering ranging from theatre and ballet to film,

music, dancing, sports, and exhibitions, rounded off with the **Musikfest Hamburg** (September, orchestral and chamber music) and the **Hamburg Ballet Season** in May / June. Proof that Hamburg also gives a high priority to sport can be found in the major international events such as the Ladies Tennis Tournament (April / May), the "German Open" international tennis championships in May (both in Rothenbaum), the international show-jumping, dressage, and four-in-hand championships (May / June in Klein Flottbek), and the Derby Week at the Hamburg- Horn race course (June / July), recently held for the 125th time. There are also innumerable sporting events such as National League football, in which Hamburg has two teams at the same time: HSV and St Pauli, to meet every taste in an enthusiastic public.

Tips and addresses from A to Z
Area code for Hamburg 040

Airport:
Airport information tel. 5075-0
www.ham.airport.de

Alster round trips:
City tours by water: 28th March-28th Sept. 10 am to 6 pm every half-hour, 29th Sept.-26th Oct. 10 am, 11 am-4 pm every half-hour, 5 pm, 27th Oct.-end March 10.30 am, 12 am, 1.30 pm, 3 pm, duration 50 min.

Boat hire *(a few examples)*
Hire of sailing and rowing boats and pedalos for a fine trip across the Alster: Bobby Reich, Fernsicht 2, tel. 487824 Alfred Seebeck, An der Alster (opposite Atlantic Hotel), tel. 247652

Casinos:
Hotel Inter-Continental,
phone 040/447044
Casino Reeperbahn, phone 040/310438

Events: *See: annual events, Page 76.*

Fish Market
Sundays 5 am-9.30 am (Nov. to March from 7 am)

Harbour tours *(various possibilities):*
with HADAG ships or motorlaunches, from St Pauli landing bridges 1-9, as well as Deichstrasse/Binnenhafen, April-Oct. every day 10 am-5.30 pm every half-hour, Nov.-March Saturdays and Sundays 11 am, 12.30 am, 2 pm, 3.30 pm, weekdays upon request, duration approx. 1 hour.
Historical Fleet Tour
From Vorsetzen April to October every day 10.30 am, 12.15 am and 4 pm, duration approx. 2 hours.

Information and hotel reservations:
Tourismus-Zentrale Hamburg GmbH,
P.O. Box 102249, 20015 Hamburg, Hamburg hotline every day 8 am-8 pm tel. 30051-3 00, www.hamburg-tourismus.de

*info@hamburg-tourismus.de or at the **Tourist Information Offices:***
Tourist information at mainline station: *main exit to Kirchenallee, Mondays to Saturdays 8 am to 9 pm, Sundays 10 am to 6 pm*
Tourist information in the port:
St. Pauli landing bridges, between bridges 4 + 5, from 1st November to 31st March every day 10 am to 6 pm, Tuesdays, Thursdays, Fridays, Saturdays 10 am to 7 pm; from 1st April to 31st October every day 8 am to 6 pm, Tuesdays, Thursdays, Fridays, Saturdays 8 am to 7 pm.
Airport office
Hamburg Airport, Terminal 4, information desk Every day 5.30 am-11 pm

Museum ships:
Windjammer Rickmer Rickmers, St. Pauli landing bridges, Bridge 1, 10 am to 6 pm every day; tel. 3195959, Cap San Diego, Überseebrücke, 10 am to 6 pm every day, tel. 364209

Planten und Blomen:
water-and-light organ, May to August, 10 pm, September 9 pm.

Public transport
Information: tel. 19449

Rathaus *(town hall)*
Guided tours of the Rathaus: Mondays to Thursdays, 10 am to 3 pm; Fridays to Sundays, 10 am to 1 pm; every half-hour. Guided tours in English and French: Mondays to Thursdays, 10.15 am to 3.15 pm; Fridays to Sundays; 10.15 am to 1.15 pm; every hour. No guided tours when official events are taking place. Information: tel. 42831-2470

Sightseeing tours *(various possibilities)*
Tickets for all sightseeing tours can be bought at the tourist information

offices

Top Tour Hamburg *April-Oct. - every day 9.30 am - 5 pm; Nov.- March, Mo-Saturdays, 11 am, 1 pm + 3 pm, Sun. 11 am + 1 pm. Duration approximately 90 minutes. You can see the most important and the most interesting sights from the Außenalster to the town centre and from St. Pauli to the port.*

Gala Tour Hamburg *every day - 10 am + 2 pm, duration 2 1/2 h. Besides the programme of the Top Tour Hamburg this tour (almost 50 kilometres long) will show you the most beautiful spots of the town such as the suburbs along the Elbe.*

Town and port combined *Both tours can be combined with a visit of the port paying an extra charge.*

Sightseeing tour by double-decker
April to October every day 9.30 am to 5 pm, every half an hour. November to March, Mondays to Fridays 10 am to 4 pm every hour, Saturdays, Sundays and public holidays 9.30 am to 4 pm every half an hour. During this tour (providing it is nice weather then with open "deck") you can get off at the most important sights and continue the trip later on. 10.30 am, 0.30 pm, 2.30 pm, 4.30 pm.

Sightseeing tour by train
April-Oct. - every day 10.30 am, 0.30 pm, 2.30 pm, Duration 105 min. A fascinating and interesting sightseeing tour on board of a "historical train" of the Twenties.

City guided tours *(on foot)*
Hamburg city tour *with the official guides of the Tourism Centre Hamburg (April to October)*

Warehouses *(typical Hamburg dock warehouses): Mondays, 4 pm, Mönckebergstrasse 3 (Kaufhof),*

duration approx 2 hours.
Speicherstadt *("warehouse city")* **and port city**, *Tuesdays, 4 pm from underground station "Baumwall" exit Speicherstadt.*
For other tours and more information please call Tourist Information Offices.

Sightseeing tour by seaplane
Tours by seaplane from Mid March, every day except Mondays, from 10 am to sunset; duration of the flight approx. 20 minutes, phone 040/378341

Theatres:
Tickets are available from travel agents via the START systems or via HAMBURG-HOTLINE. Tel. 30051300.

Trade fairs and exhibitions:
Hamburg Messe und Congress GmbH, tel. 3569-0

Youth hostels:
Stintfang youth hostel, Alfred Wegener Weg 5, 20459 Hamburg, tel. 31 34 88; Hamburg young people's hotel "Horner Rennbahn", Rennbahnstrasse 100, 22111 Hamburg, tel. 6511671.

Waxworks
Exhibition with more than 120 famous persons from history to politics, sport and showbusiness, Mondays to Fridays 11 am to 9 pm, Saturdays 11 am to 12 pm, Sundays 10 am to 9 pm.

Zoo:
Hagenbeck's Zoo, tel. 54000147, from 9 am onwards every day.

Further guides published by Kraichgau Verlag

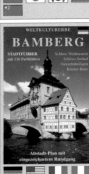

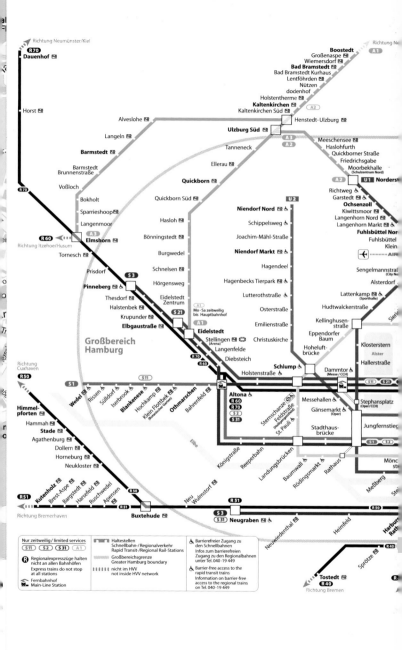

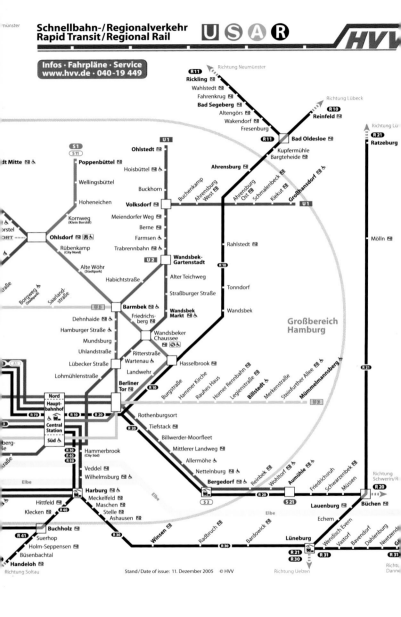

Schnellbahn-/Regionalverkehr
Rapid Transit/Regional Rail U S A R ⟋HVV

Infos · Fahrpläne · Service
www.hvv.de · 040-19 449

Richtung Neumünster

R11 Rickling
Wahlstedt
Fahrenkrug
Bad Segeberg
Altengörs
Wakendorf
Fresenburg
R11

Richtung Lübeck

R10 Reinfeld

Bad Oldesloe
Kupfermühle
Bargteheide

Richtung Lü

R21 Ratzeburg

S1
S11
U1 Ohlstedt
Poppenbüttel
Hoisbüttel
Wellingsbüttel
Buckhorn
Hoheneichen
Volksdorf
Kornweg (Klein Borstel)
Meiendorfer Weg
Berne
Farmsen
Trabrennbahn

dt Mitte
Ahrensburg

Buchenkamp
Ahrensburg West
Ahrensburg Ost
Schmalenbeck
Kiekut
Großhansdorf U1

orstel
Ohlsdorf U⬤
Rübenkamp (City Nord)

Mölln

Alte Wöhr (Stadtpark)
U2 Wandsbek-Gartenstadt
Alter Teichweg
Straßburger Straße

Rahlstedt

Tonndorf

Großbereich
Hamburg

ße
Borgweg (Stadtpark)
Saarlandstraße
Habichtstraße

Barmbek
Wandsbek Markt

Wandsbek

Dehnhaide
Friedrichsberg
Hamburger Straße
Wandsbeker Chaussee
Mundsburg
Uhlandstraße
Lübecker Straße
Ritterstraße
Wartenau
Hasselbrook

R21

Lohmühlenstraße
Landwehr
Berliner Tor

Burgstraße
Hammer Kirche
Rauhes Haus
Horner Rennbahn
Legienstraße
Billstedt
Merkenstraße
Steinfurther Allee
Mümmelmannsberg
U3

Nord
Hauptbahnhof
Central Station
Süd

R70 R10 R20

Rothenburgsort
Tiefstack
Billwerder-Moorfleet
Mittlerer Landweg
Allermöhe
Nettelnburg
Bergedorf

Reinbek
Wohltorf
Aumühle
Friedrichsruh
Schwarzenbek
Müssen

Richtung Schwerin/R

R20 Büchen

bergse
Hammerbrook (City Süd)
Veddel
Wilhelmsburg

R30 R40 R50

R20 S21 Lauenburg

Elbe

Harburg
Meckelfeld
Maschen
Stelle
Ashausen

S2

Echem

traße
Hittfeld
Klecken

R40

Elbe

Lüneburg

Buchholz
R41 Suerhop
Holm-Seppensen
Büsenbachtal
Handeloh

R30

Winsen
Radbruch
Bardowick

Lüneburg

Wendisch Evern
Vastorf
Bavendorf
Dahlenburg
Neetzend

R21
R30
R31
R31

Richtung Soltau

Richti
Danne

Stand/Date of issue: 11. Dezember 2005   © HVV

Richtung Uelzen